P9-AOK-735

JAPANESE ONE-POT COOKERY

The medallion on the jacket is a reproduction of the Bronze Medals awarded the four cookbooks in this set, Rice Recipes from Around the World, Cook Japanese, Cook Chinese, Japanese One-Pot Cookery, *by the Gastronomic Academy of Germany on the occasion of the 12th International Culinary Art Exhibition (1968).*

日本の鍋料理

JAPANESE ONE-POT COOKERY

By MASARU DOI

Photographs by
YOSHIKATSU SAEKI

KODANSHA INTERNATIONAL LTD: PUBLISHERS
Tokyo, Japan   Palo Alto, California, U.S.A.

DISTRIBUTORS:

British Commonwealth (excluding Canada and the Far East)
WARD LOCK & COMPANY LTD.
London and Sydney

Continental Europe
BOXERBOOKS, INC.
Zurich

The Far East
JAPAN PUBLICATIONS TRADING COMPANY
C.P.O. Box 722, Tokyo

Published by KODANSHA INTERNATIONAL LTD., 2-12-21, Otowa,
Bunkyo-ku, Tokyo, Japan and KODANSHA INTERNATIONAL/USA
LTD., 577 College Avenue, Palo Alto, California 94306. Copyright
© in Japan, 1966, by KODANSHA INTERNATIONAL LTD. All rights
reserved. Printed in Japan.
Library of Congress Catalog Card No. 67-12410
S.B.N. 87011-123-X J.B.C. 2377-781482-2361
First edition, 1966
Revised edition, 1970
Second printing, 1970

Table of Contents

Preface

DURING MY SEVERAL trips to the United States and Europe, I especially appreciated invitations to parties at private homes. The warm hospitality offered by friends in foreign lands remains in the heart of a lonesome traveler. Always of particular interest to me are the foods served at such parties. Food always reflects the tradition and taste of the people. The menus of various countries may differ, but the friendliness of the people and the atmosphere of parties at home are the same everywhere.

In Japan, the spirit of *wa* (unity and harmony) is held in high esteem. Relations between members of the family and friends are highly regarded, and occasions to enhance ties are always sought.

The recipes introduced in this book are intended for such parties. When several people gather around a pot to cook, converse, eat and drink, the atmosphere is bound to become as friendly and enjoyable as the food will be delicious.

Equipment and materials for Japanese cookery are being exported in great quantities and it has become a pleasant diversion to have a party "à la japonaise." I have adapted some of the recipes for the convenience of the Western cook and have added variations in an attempt to solve the problem of obtaining ingredients.

It gives me great pleasure to feel that some of these recipes might be prepared by the warm fireside in the winter or at an outdoor gathering in a distant land.

I express my sincere appreciation to Mrs. Marilyn Mihal, who edited the English text of this book.

I am greatly indebted to the staff of Kodansha International who have made this publication possible and lastly wish to thank the readers of my previous book, *Cook Japanese*, by the same publisher, which has been so well received.

July, 1966

MASARU DOI

[NOTE: The recipes in this book are designed to serve four persons.]

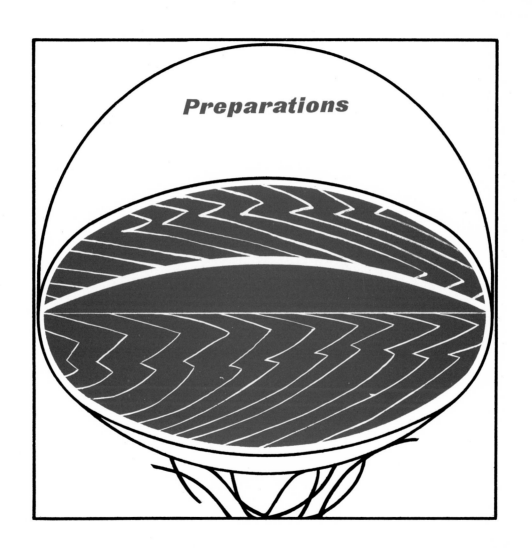

Nabé-mono

A NABÉ is a pot. Usually. It is also a stew kettle and a skillet and a casserole and a pan. Confusing? How much simpler to have just one word for almost every kind of cooking container. And how convenient to entertain family and friends with a whole meal cooked in just one pot! It's an old Japanese custom.

Nabé-mono literally means "pot-things," but as everyone who has traveled in Japan knows, the lavish variety of nabé-mono is enjoyed everywhere—from the farmhouse to the most exclusive restaurant; truly, the word is best translated as the art of one-pot cookery.

Nabé-mono, these bountiful one-pot dishes, are very popular winter fare in Japan. The charm of gathering around a charcoal (or any other) cooker and partaking of flavorful morsels, accompanied by steaming hot soup, is readily apparent in a land where central heating is the exception.

Such a convivial scene need not be limited to Japan. The cooking of a beautiful array of ingredients is done before the diners' eyes—and sometimes with their participation—making it perfect party fare or a treat for the family. One-pot nabé-mono cookery is adaptable to any number of guests, and the variety of ingredients is designed to please everyone. Since the initial preparation can be done well beforehand, nabé-mono allows the hostess to spend most of her time with her guests.

Choice of Utensils

SINCE MOST of these dishes are both cooked and served at the table, the choice of utensils plays an exceedingly important role in making the meal attractive. Fortunately, a large variety of attractive cooking utensils is available.

A wide, shallow pot (casserole, skillet, etc.), heavy enough to hold the heat, is best for cooking over direct heat. The size is important, too, and should be gauged to the number of people to be served—a small pot is usually sufficient for two or three persons. If you plan to serve more than eight, it would be preferable to use two containers (and a heat source for each).

Sukiyaki Skillets

Sizes:	iron skillet –	10″ (diameter)	serves	3–4
		12″	,,	5–6
		14″	,,	7–8
	earthenware pot –	7″	serves	2
		10″	,,	3
		10″	,,	4–5
		12″	,,	6–8

IRON SKILLETS

An iron skillet should be heavy and thick, especially at the bottom, in order to conduct and maintain even heat. A thin skillet heats unevenly and tends to burn food quickly. Iron skillets are generally used for those dishes that require only a small amount of liquid, such as *suki-yaki* or *teppan-yaki*.

Treatment

To remove the metallic taste and traces of oil from the skillet, first wash it well with soap and water, rinse, and then boil water and leftover vegetables in it. Empty, rinse and use. After use, bring water to a boil in it, clean well and dry thoroughly. Oil inside before storing it.

Boiling Pots   **Ghenghis Khan Griddle**   **Teppan Griddle**

Types
(1) *Sukiyaki skillet*. A round cast-iron pan, thick at the bottom. Some have a depression in the center to gather meat juices.
(2) *Boiling pot*. A large, deep pot for those dishes using a large amount of thin broth. (Earthenware casseroles are also used for these dishes.)
(3) *Ghenghis Khan griddle*. A special type of skillet used for grilling. The center is dome-shaped with incised gutters that allow juices to run down and collect around the edges of the dome.
(4) *Teppan griddle*. A square, flat griddle with slightly raised edges. Both meats and vegetables can be grilled on it.

EARTHENWARE POTS
This simple shape is very familiar in Japan. Its capacity to hold heat makes it particularly suitable for stewing and the cooking of *nabé-mono*.

Treatment
These pots are usually soft, low-fired earthenware. Consequently they are fragile in spite of their heavy appearance and require special treatment.

Before using for the first time, clean inside thoroughly, fill with water and let stand for 20–30 minutes. Wipe off any drops of water that have formed on the outside, bring to a boil slowly over low heat, and allow to simmer for 5–6 hours, adding more water when necessary. Cool

Earthernware Pots

  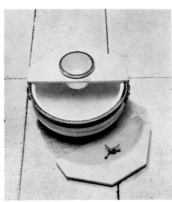 

and use. Never start cooking over high heat or place the empty pot on the heat. Avoid getting the outside, and especially the bottom, wet. After use, wash only the inside. If a new earthenware pot has an odor, this can be removed by boiling coarse green tea *(bancha)* in it. If it should crack, cook rice or rice gruel in it to seal the cracks.

STAINLESS STEEL PANS
These are easy to care for, but tend to cook food quickly, increasing the danger of cooking dry and burning. They are useful for dishes cooked in a quantity of soup, such as *yudofu* or *oden*.

ALUMINUM PANS
A thick one is preferable. It conducts heat quickly but does not retain it well.

CHINA
Special sets of china for serving *nabé-mono* are sold in Japan. These usually consist of a large bowl, small individual bowls, spice containers and a *ponzu* sauce cup.

COOKING AT THE TABLE:
Any type of burner that can be used at the table may be used—a gas ring, electric hotplate, or charcoal-burning hibachi. A heavy chafing dish (with strong heating capacity) or an electric skillet or saucepan may also be used.

あすか鍋

ASUKA NABÉ—A COZY EVENING'S TREAT

GENERAL HINTS ABOUT INGREDIENTS

(1) All ingredients should be cut into desired sizes beforehand. Arrange them in a pleasing manner on a large platter or tray—with as much care as you would use in making a flower arrangement. The visual impact of this "picture" increases anticipation among your guests and adds an esthetic dimension to the occasion.

(2) Wash vegetables well beforehand to allow ample time for thorough draining prior to use.

(3) Use meat and vegetables in proportions that assure nutritive balance—at least two parts assorted vegetables to one part meat.

(4) With fish, savory vegetables such as chopped leek and watercress enhance the flavor.

(5) To subdue the strong aroma of mutton, rub it with garlic, grated ginger root or bean paste.

(6) Vegetables that require longer cooking, such as potatoes, carrots, *daikon* or turnips, should be parboiled in advance.

(7) Since spinach and *shungiku* have a rather harsh flavor, they may be boiled briefly before using. They are often parboiled and rolled together with Chinese cabbage and then sliced, producing an attractive design.

(8) *Konnyaku* should be rubbed well with salt, pounded lightly with a wooden pestle, and parboiled.

(9) Pour hot water over *abura-age* to remove excess oil.

(10) Dried vegetables such as mushrooms should be washed and then soaked in warm water until tender. Save this water for use in soup stock.

鉄板焼

TEPPAN-YAKI
BY THE LAKESIDE

COOKING HINTS

(1) Heat should be controlled with regard to the various ingredients. In *nabé-mono*, heat should be lowered when soup reaches the boiling point to prevent stock from evaporating and foodstuffs from losing shape.

(2) Fish fillet should be cooked at the beginning so that it will lend its flavor to the soup. Eat fish and meat as soon as they are done to your satisfaction. They will toughen if left in too long.

(3) Start with those ingredients that require the longest cooking time, adding the others later.

(4) Avoid overcooking *tofu* or it will harden and develop holes.

(5) Overcooking will decrease the flavor of *shungiku* and trefoil and make the broth "muddy," so these should be eaten as soon as they are cooked.

(6) When serving *nabé-mono*, eat foods as they are cooked, remembering to replace them with additional fresh ingredients to be cooked. Add sauce, soup stock or water when needed to maintain an adequate amount.

(7) Each guest may help himself from the pot, using chopsticks. The opposite end of one's chopsticks can be used to remove food from the pot.

おでん

**HOTCHPOTCH
AND FISH—
A FIRESIDE DELIGHT**

TIMING

IT IS important, in the preparation of *nabé-mono*, to consider the timing of each ingredient cooked. These dishes differ from most Western casseroles in that all of the ingredients are not cooked together for a given length of time and then eaten, but are added throughout the meal as soon as the previous round is eaten. They are "convivial" dishes—and when conversation becomes lively and eating is temporarily neglected, it is wise to add only those ingredients, such as mushrooms and leeks, that will not suffer from overcooking.

In bubbling *tofu*, the tofu should be served when it first sways in the broth. In *chiri-nabé*, fish fillet is ready to eat as soon as it changes color, and the greens need be turned only once. It will soon become apparent to you that the minimum cooking time is best in most cases. Flavor, texture and food value are at their peak!

やきとり

**SKEWERED
CHICKEN
PICNIC**

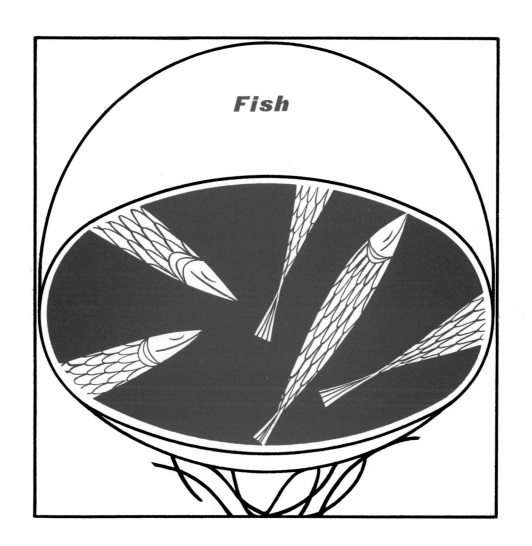

YOSE-NABÉ

YOSE-NABÉ means "a gathering of everything," and is one of Japan's most popular *nabé* dishes. The flavor of this assortment of fresh seafood and vegetables will explain its popularity.

Ingredients

3 onions, 2 quartered and 1 diced

1 large tomato (4 oz.). Core, submerge in hot water for 30–40 seconds, rinse in cold water, peel, remove seeds and dice.

1 live spring lobster (1½ lbs.). Cut off head and section body.

1 lb. sea bream fillet, cut into 1″ cubes

8 medium clams, soaked in salt water (2 Tbsps. salt per 5 cups water) for 3–4 hours. Wash in fresh water to remove slippery film from shells.

1 carrot, sliced diagonally while turning carrot with left hand, parboiled

1 head cabbage (1 lb.), quartered along core

1 piece ginger root, peeled and minced

1 Tbsp. vegetable oil

Seasoning: ½ cup *saké*; 1 tsp. salt; 1 Tbsp. light soy sauce

Method

Heat oil in skillet, sauté diced onion over high heat, stirring quickly to avoid burning, until tender. Lower heat to medium, add tomato and sauté. When tomato loses shape, add other ingredients (except cabbage) and add water barely to cover (about 6 cups), raising heat to bring to a boil. Skim off foam and floating fat thoroughly when it boils up. Add ½ cup *saké*, lower heat and simmer for 10 minutes. Add cabbage and cook another 7—8 minutes or until tender. Season with 1 tsp. salt and 1 Tbsp. light soy sauce, adding more salt if necessary. Remove a selection of food to each bowl and eat with some of the broth. A squeeze of lemon juice or a dash of pepper may be added if desired.

Notes

Be sure to lower heat when broth reaches the boiling point and continue to skim off the foam as the broth simmers.

Variations

Prawns, flounder, or any white meat fish fillet may be added. Curry powder may be used as a seasoning. In this as in most *nabé-mono*, ingredients may be varied according to season and availability.

よせ鍋

YOSE-NABÉ

23

TEMPURA

TEMPURA is enjoyed far beyond the shores of Japan, but it is often limited to shrimp and a few vegetables. Surprise your guests with the variety offered in this recipe—and since each morsel is skewered, they can participate in the cooking if they like. Incidentally, the secret of good *tempura* lies in eating it as soon as it is cooked.

Ingredients

$\frac{1}{4}$ lb. lean beef (sirloin or tenderloin), diced in $\frac{1}{2}''$ cubes

$\frac{1}{4}$ lb.white meat fish fillet (sea bream, flounder, etc.), sliced $\frac{1}{2}''$ thick

8 shrimps, shelled (leaving tail intact), and black veins removed

8 green chili peppers, seeded

1 sweet potato ($\frac{1}{2}$ lb.), sliced $\frac{1}{4}''$ thick, with peel

4 stalks asparagus, tough ends discarded, cut into 2″ lengths

2 stalks celery, strung and cut into 2″ lengths

4 small onions, peeled and halved

4 canned sweet chestnuts, drained

Spear each of the above ingredients individually on a bamboo skewer.

Tempura batter (see basic recipe)

Spices: *momiji-oroshi* (see basic recipe)
        sarashi-negi (see basic recipe)

Tempura sauce (2 cups) (see basic recipe)

3–4 cups oil for deep frying. Flavor with sesame oil if available.

Method

Fill a deep frying pan $\frac{3}{4}$ full with oil (a fondue pot is even better), and heat to 340°–350°F. This should be prepared at the table so that foods can be served and eaten as soon as they are done. Flour each of the skewered pieces, dip in batter and deep fry for 1–2 minutes. Each guest should have a small bowl of *tempura* sauce with his choice of spices as dip.

Notes

Too many pieces cooked at one time will lower the oil temperature and cause the batter to be glutinous. When oil is too hot, ingredients will burn before they are thoroughly cooked. Ingredients that require a longer cooking time (such as sweet potato, onion, etc.) should be deep fried at a lower temperature (340°) for 5–6 minutes. Avoid keeping the batter too close to the heat when not in use or it will thicken.

Variations

Sprinkle with sesame seeds, or use cocktail sauce or tartar sauce as a dip. Also, try dipping the various ingredients in batter and then dredge with crumbs, chopped *harusame* (transparent vermicelli) or vermicelli (uncooked) before deep frying.

天ぷら

TEMPURA

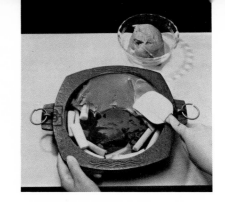

OYSTER NABÉ (Kaki Dote-nabé)

THIS DISH is prepared with a bank of bean paste lining the sides of the casserole. The bean paste melts into the soup giving a unique flavor to the ingredients.

Ingredients

1 lb. large oysters, gently washed in lightly salted water to remove bits of shell or sand, drained

1 loaf roasted *tofu* (bean curd, 1½ lbs.) diced into 1″ cubes

½ lb. *shungiku*, roots removed, divided into uniform-sized sprigs

2 stalks leek, cut into 1½″ lengths. (Western leeks are much thicker and should be quartered lengthwise.)

Bean paste: Mix 2 oz. red bean paste and 9 oz. white bean paste with 5 Tbsps. *mirin*.

4 eggs (1 as a dip for each guest)

1 cup soup stock

Method

Line sides of an earthenware pot or iron skillet with half of the leek, spread mixed bean paste on leek with rubber spatula, forming a bank (see process illustration). Arrange the remaining leek, roasted *tofu*, oysters and *shungiku* attractively in the center.

Place over a low flame and pour in half of the soup stock. When soup comes to a boil, turn over the *tofu* and add the remaining stock gradually. As soon as the oysters swell and their edges curl, dip into beaten egg and eat.

Notes

Scorching the bean paste a bit at first will increase the flavor. When the bean paste melts, add soup stock gradually. Be careful not to overcook the oysters or they will toughen and lose flavor. The ratio of the two kinds of bean paste may be changed according to taste.

Variations

Instead of *mirin*, *saké* may be used, adding 3 Tbsps. sugar. Other shellfish, with shells removed, may be substituted for oysters.

かき土手鍋

OYSTER NABÉ (Kaki Dote-nabé)

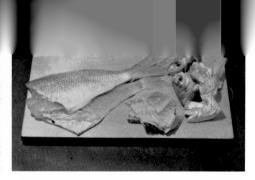

CHIRI-NABÉ OF SEA BREAM

THIS IS a delightful way of preparing sea bream—and any white meat fish responds equally well to this treatment.

Ingredients

1 whole sea bream (3½ lbs.) or other white meat fish. Clean and fillet (see instructions and process illustrations). Slice into 1″ slices. Cut head and center bone into fairly large pieces, pour boiling water over them, wash thoroughly in cold water, and drain.

4 stalks leek, cut into 1½″ lengths

4 large mushrooms, washed, stemmed and halved

1½ loaves *tofu*, cut into 1″ cubes

1 head Chinese cabbage (1½ lbs.)

½ lb. spinach

Parboil both cabbage and spinach, roll together with spinach in the center (see basic recipe) and cut into 1″ widths.

¼ lb. *shungiku*, roots discarded, separated into sprigs

2 oz. *harusame*, soaked in lukewarm water for 5–6 minutes and cut into 2″ lengths

Arrange ingredients decoratively on a large platter.

1 sheet *konbu* (6″ square). Sponge both sides with a damp cloth and make slits across fibers but not through to edges.

Spices: *momiji-oroshi* (see basic recipe)
　　　 sarashi-negi (see basic recipe)

Ponzu sauce (see basic recipe)

Method

Put *konbu* in earthenware pot ⅔ full of water, set on medium heat and remove *konbu* just before the boiling point is reached. Put in the head and center bone with a part of the flesh, and lower heat when it comes to a boil again. Simmer for 4–5 minutes, skimming off foam and floating fat. Transfer the casserole to a heating unit on the table. (If you like, remove the head and bones first.) Add leek and mushrooms, cook until tender and add a portion of the remaining ingredients. Add more as these are eaten. Individual cups of *ponzu* sauce with a little of the spices should be provided as dip.

Notes

Choose only fresh fish. Pork or chicken fillet may be added. Do not forget to skim off foam while cooking.

たいちり

CHIRI-NABÉ OF
SEA BREAM

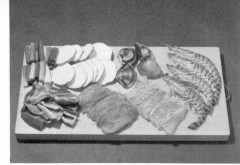

TEPPAN-YAKI

THIS DISH is named after the iron griddle on which it is prepared. Delightful fare when cooked at the table, it also makes an interesting variation for an outdoor barbeque.

Ingredients

$\frac{1}{2}$ lb. beef (sirloin or tenderloin), sliced $\frac{1}{4}''$ thick

$\frac{1}{2}$ lb. white meat fish fillet (sea bream, whitefish, etc.) sliced $\frac{1}{2}''$ thick

4 large clams, soaked in lightly salted water ($1\frac{1}{2}$ tsp. to 1 cup water) for 4–5 hours. Cut ligaments (see basic recipe, page 102) to prevent clams from opening when cooked, losing their savory juices.

4 prawns (2 oz. each), cleaned, heads removed, deveined

1 sweet potato (1/2 lb.), cut into $\frac{1}{2}''$ slices

4 bell peppers, stemmed, seeded and cut into quarters

2 stalks leek, cut into 2" lengths

3–4 Tbsps. vegetable oil

Spices: *momiji-oroshi* (see basic recipe)
        sarashi-negi (see basic recipe)

Ponzu sauce (see basic recipe)

2 Tbsps. sesame seeds, parched in dry skillet with salt

Hot sauce: Mix 1 Tbsp. dry mustard with $\frac{1}{3}$ cup *sanbai-zu* (see basic recipe)

Ketchup sauce: Mix 2 Tbsps. Worcestershire sauce, $\frac{1}{2}$ cup tomato ketchup, 2 tsps. mustard and 2 tsps. lemon juice.

Method

Heat griddle at the table and apply oil. Bring ingredients to the table attractively arranged on a large platter. Sauté ingredients until partially cooked, turn over and continue until done. Clams and prawns should be done over medium heat for 7–8 minutes, turning once. Serve and eat while hot, with the sauce and spice of your choice.

Notes

Choose the freshest possible fish and shellfish. Do not overcook ingredients or they will lose flavor. The griddle should be thick and heavy. A heavy frying pan or large, shallow pan may be substituted if it is attractive enough to bring to the table.

Variations

Oysters, chicken, pork or mushrooms may be added.

 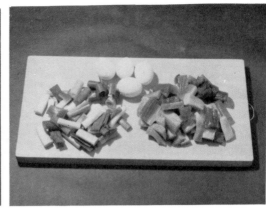

FRESH TUNA AND LEEK NABÉ (Negima-nabé)

A DELICIOUS and extremely simple way of preparing fresh tuna.

Ingredients

1½ lbs. tuna, cut into pieces 1½″ × 1″ × ½″

4 stalks thick leek, cut into 1½″ lengths. Halve thick part.

4 eggs, for dip

Seasoning: 5 Tbsps. *saké*; ½ cup soy sauce; 4 Tbsps. sugar

Spices: powdered *sansho* or 7-flavors pepper

Method

Boil 2 cups water with seasoning in skillet, lower heat and add tuna and leek. When tuna changes color, turn over and cook for 1–2 minutes. Prepare beaten egg, sprinkle with 7-flavors pepper or *sansho* and use as dip. Serve hot.

Notes

Arrange ingredients on a large platter with mixed seasonings close at hand. Cook about half of the ingredients, then add the remainder while these are being eaten. Choose the fat part of the tuna, since the lean will harden and dry out when cooked in this manner.

Variations

Savory vegetables like trefoil or watercress may be added. If you prefer, use mustard as the spice. In place of tuna, yellowtail may be used.

32

ねぎま鍋

**FRESH TUNA
AND LEEK NABÉ
(Negima-nabé)**

CRAB CRADLE NABÉ (Kani Miso-nabé)

A MIXTURE of bean paste and crab roe gives this dish its distinctive flavor.

Ingredients

1 boiled crab (about 3½ lbs.). Remove roe from shell (reserve both) and cut legs from body. Cut these diagonally into pieces to facilitate eating.

3 stalks leek, cut diagonally into 2½" lengths

1½ loaves *konnyaku*, rubbed well with salt, lightly pounded with wooden pestle, and washed

1 loaf *tofu*, cut into 1" cubes

3 oz. string beans. String, boil for 2–3 minutes in water with a pinch of salt, rinse in cold water and cut in two, if long.

5 Tbsps. red bean paste, mixed well with crab roe and packed into crab shell

5 cups soup stock or broth

Arrange above ingredients decoratively in large casserole.

Seasoning: 2 cups *saké*; 3 Tbsps. sugar; 2 Tbsps. soy sauce

Method

Put casserole over heat and gently pour in soup stock or broth. When bean paste in shell melts, add seasonings (above). Serve and eat as ingredients are cooked, adding some of the soup to each bowl with the ingredients. A dash of white pepper or 7-flavors pepper, or, if you prefer, grated ginger root may be added by the guests.

Notes

Rub *konnyaku* well with salt to remove excess water, and it will tighten and increase in flavor.

Variations

When live crab is used, cook over medium heat in seasoned soup for a longer period of time.

かにのみそ鍋

CRAB CRADLE NABÉ (Kani Miso-nabé)

35

SALMON NABÉ (Ishikari-nabè)

THIS DISH takes its name from the place in Hokkaido (northernmost island of Japan) where it originated. Seafood is plentiful and good there, and the people of the area are expert in preparing it.

Ingredients

1 whole salmon (3½ lbs.), head removed, washed well and cut into ½" slices

2 loaves *tofu*, diced into 1" cubes

1 head Chinese cabbage (2 lbs.)

½ lb. spinach

Boil both cabbage and spinach, spread on bamboo mat in alternate layers, making *hakata* (see basic recipe), and cut into 1" widths.

8 mushrooms, washed, stemmed and halved, if large

5 oz. *shungiku*, washed. Discard roots and separate tender parts into uniform sprigs.

5 cups soup stock, seasoned with 5 Tbsps. sugar, ½ cup soy sauce

Method

Bring seasoned soup stock to boil, add salmon and cook for 3–4 minutes over medium heat, skimming off foam as it forms. Cook *tofu*, Chinese cabbage, mushrooms and *shungiku*; serve and eat with broth.

Notes

Cook over medium heat. Choose fresh salmon. Add raw ingredients to pot only as cooked ingredients are eaten, saving ⅓ of the soup stock to be added as needed. Be sure to keep soup boiling while cooking. Do not overcook greens and *tofu*.

Variations

If you prefer, use lemon juice, *sansho*, or 7-flavors pepper for added flavor. Boiled *daikon*, *konnyaku* or leek may be added.

石狩鍋

SALMON NABÉ
(Ishikari-nabé)

PRAWN NUGGET NABÉ (Ebi Dango-nabé)

THESE BALLS of ground prawn are particularly luscious.

Ingredients

2 lbs. (including shells) prawns, 1 egg, 3 Tbsps. flour.
Remove heads and shells from prawns, mince and
grind well. Mix with beaten egg, flour, and season
with 1 tsp. salt, 2 tsps. *mirin*, and a pinch of monosodium glutamate.

1 head of Chinese cabbage (2 lbs.)
Separate leaves, parboil, a small quantity at a time,
in 1 cup water in a tightly covered pan (see basic
recipe), drain, sprinkle with salt and let cool.

8 dried mushrooms, soaked to soften, stems removed

5 oz. trefoil, cut into 2″ lengths

6 cups soup stock, seasoned with ½ cup soy sauce, ⅓ cup
mirin

Method

Bring soup to boil, lower heat. Squeeze prawn mixture
(see process illustration) into bite-sized balls, drop into
soup and cook for 4–5 minutes, skimming off foam as
it forms on the soup. Add remaining ingredients except
trefoil, cook for 5–6 minutes over medium heat, and
remove to table. Strew trefoil over top, ladle out ingredients with broth into individual bowls and serve
hot.

Notes

Cooking over strong heat will cause prawn balls to
swell and become coarse in texture.

Variations

Try fish or chicken balls in place of prawn. Sliced ham
may be added.

えび団子鍋

PRAWN NUGGET NABÉ (Ebi Dango-nabé)

TREASURE AND PLEASURE NABÉ
(Horaku-nabé)

AN ASSORTMENT of seafood, baked in a unique manner on a bed of pebbles and pine needles. Your guests will be intrigued!

Ingredients

  4 prawns (2 oz. each), washed in lightly salted water, black veins removed with a bamboo skewer

  10 oz. sea bream or yellowtail cut into 4 pieces. Make decorative scores crosswise on skin (see process illustration), salt lightly.

  4 clams (large), soaked in lightly salted water for 5–6 hours. Cut ligaments to prevent them from opening and losing juice, and sprinkle salt over shells.

  8 canned sweet chestnuts, drained

  12 gingko nuts. Crack shells and roast.

  Ponzu sauce (for 4) (see basic recipe)

  Pebbles, pine needles, salt

Method

  Place a layer of pebbles in the bottom of an earthenware pot or *horaku-nabé* (iron or glass ovenware can be used), cover with pine needles (see process illustration) and arrange prawns, sea bream, clams, chestnuts and gingko nuts in a decorative manner and cover. Place in a medium oven (350° F.) for 10 minutes, remove cover, raise heat (415°) and bake for another 7–8 minutes. Serve hot with *ponzu* sauce for dip.

Notes

  Pebbles prevent the food from being stained with burning juice, and the heat through the layer of pebbles cooks very gently. Unless prawns are strictly fresh, remove the heads.

Variations

  Steam same ingredients over high heat, covering bottom of pot with *konbu* instead of the pebbles and pine needles. Eat with lemon juice and salt.

宝楽鍋

**TREASURE AND PLEASURE
NABÉ**

(Horaku-nabé)

SEAFOOD SUKIYAKI (Uo-suki)

AN INTERESTING and delicious variation of the ever-popular *sukiyaki*—made with a selection of seafood instead of the usual beef.

Ingredients

11 oz. flounder or yellowtail, sliced ½" thick

11 oz. sea bream, boned, sliced ½" thick

11 oz. cuttlefish, thin skin thoroughly removed (rubbing with a wet cloth is helpful if this proves difficult), scored lengthwise

4 prawns (2 oz. each), shelled (leaving head and tail intact), black veins removed

4 mushrooms (large), cleaned, stemmed and halved

1 head Chinese cabbage, cut into 1" slices. Halve large leaves lengthwise.

2 bunches trefoil (3 oz.), roots removed, cut into 1½" lengths

1 stick roasted *fu*, cut into 1" lengths, soaked in water to soften and pressed to drain

9 oz. *shirataki*, cut into 2" lengths, lightly boiled and drained

1 loaf *tofu*, cut into 1" cubes

Arrange all ingredients except fish and shellfish attractively on a large platter.

Sauce: Mix ½ cup soup stock, ½ cup *mirin*, ½ cup soy sauce, and 3 Tbsps. sugar. Marinate white meat fish, sea bream, cuttlefish and prawns in sauce for 3–4 minutes before cooking.

4 eggs, for dip

Method

Pour marinade into skillet, place over fire, and when marinade starts to boil, add the fish. When edges of the fish turn white, turn and continue to cook for 5 minutes. Eat, dipping into beaten egg. Add vegetables and *tofu* a bit at a time and eat as soon as they are cooked.

Notes

When broth cooks away, add soup stock or *saké* to taste. Do not marinate fish too long or it will mask individual flavors. Since fish fillet is easily broken, do not stir while cooking. When prawns are not strictly fresh, remove the heads, wash in lightly salted water, and shell, leaving the tail intact.

Variations

Add other fresh fish such as yellowtail. *Shungiku* and fresh mushrooms may be used in season.

魚すき

SEAFOOD SUKIYAKI (Uo-suki)
43

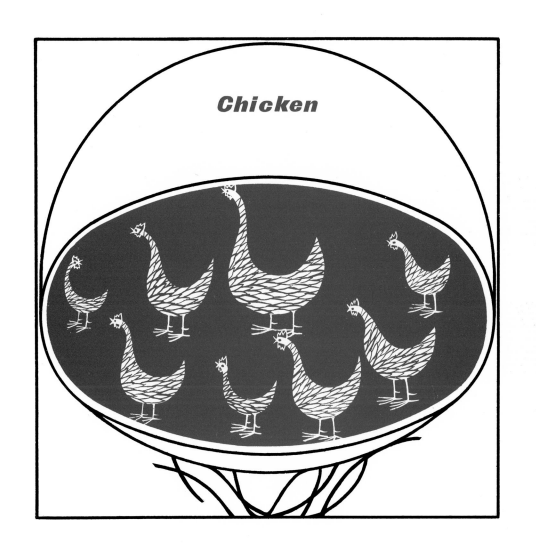

MIZUTAKI OF CHICKEN

THIS IS popular in Japan—and deservedly so. The broth is rich and flavorful and the morsels of chicken and vegetables, dipped into the *ponzu* sauce, are very tasty.

Ingredients

1 whole chicken (3 lbs.), chopped, bones and all, into 1″ pieces. Place chicken in casserole with 12 cups of water, bring to a boil and simmer for 1 hour over medium heat. Completely remove floating foam.

2 lbs. Chinese cabbage. Separate leaves, steam in 1 cup water, tightly covered, for 3 minutes; turn over and steam another 3 minutes. Remove, sprinkle with salt and cool. Cut into 1½″ widths.

3 stalks leek, cut into 1½″ lengths

2 loaves *tofu* (1½ lbs.), cut into 1″ cubes

2 bunches trefoil, cut into 1½″ lengths

Spices: *momiji-oroshi* (see basic recipe)
        sarashi-negi (see basic recipe)

Ponzu sauce (see basic recipe)

Method

Place cooked chicken, vegetables and *tofu* in casserole, add chicken stock and bring to a boil. Serve and eat when vegetables are tender, using spiced *ponzu* as dip. If you like, pour soup into separate bowls, add a pinch of salt, and drink.

Notes

Cook chicken over medium heat. Cooking over low heat will cause flavor loss and cooking over a high flame will harden the meat and decrease the flavor.

Variations

Try, as in *chiri-nabé* of chicken, adding rice or ricecakes to leftover soup. Add seasoning, cover with a thin layer of beaten egg and a sprinkling of chopped leek, and cook.

水たき

MIZUTAKI OF CHICKEN

ASUKA-NABÉ

ASUKA IS a historical site in Nara, from which this delicious chicken dish derives its name.

Ingredients

1½ lbs. spring chicken, boned and cut into 1″ pieces. Chicken bones, cleaned. (Cut bones into sections, pour hot water over them, wash and rinse thoroughly.) Cook bones in 5 cups water, lowering heat just before the boiling point is reached, and simmer for 30 minutes. Remove foam and scum thoroughly, and strain through a cooking cloth.

8 mushrooms, cleaned and stemmed

1 carrot, sliced diagonally into 2″ pieces (cut diagonally while turning carrot with the other hand—like sharpening a pencil), and parboiled

½ lb. *shirataki*, cut into sections, parboiled, drained

1 small head Chinese cabbage (2 lbs.), steamed

½ lb. spinach, steamed and rinsed quickly to maintain green color. Place spinach on cabbage and roll (see process illustration, page 101). Cut into 1″ slices.

3 cups milk

Seasoning: 2 tsps. salt; 1 Tbsp. light soy sauce; ½ tsp. sugar

Method

Pour stock from chicken bones (about 3 cups) into casserole, add chicken fillet and rolled cabbage and cook for 3–4 minutes. Remove foam from top and flavor with milk, salt, soy sauce and sugar. Add mushrooms and carrot, and cook for 5–6 minutes over medium heat. Remove cooked food to individual bowls and eat with broth. Sprinkle with pepper if you like.

Notes

Be sure to cook over medium heat, since cooking over high heat tends to cause the milk to separate.

Variations

Crab meat, pheasant or pigeon meat may be used in place of chicken.

あすか鍋

ASUKA-NABÉ
49

CHIRI-NABÉ OF CHICKEN

THIS DIFFERS both in taste and texture from *chiri-nabé* of sea bream, but it is equally good.

Ingredients

1 whole chicken (about 3 lbs.), disjointed and chopped into 1″ pieces

4 mushrooms (large), cleaned, stemmed and cut into wedges

1 loaf *tofu*, cut into 1″ cubes

1 small head Chinese cabbage (1½ lbs.), halved lengthwise, cored and cut into 1½″ slices crosswise

3 stalks leek, cut into 1½″ lengths

3 oz. *harusame*, soaked in lukewarm water until tender and cut into manageable lengths

1 sheet *konbu* (6″ square), slit crosswise across fibers but not through to edges

Spices: *momiji-oroshi* (see basic recipe)
        sarashi-negi (see basic recipe)

Ponzu sauce (see basic recipe)

Method

Fill casserole ¾ full with water, add *konbu*, bring to a boil and remove *konbu*. Put in chicken, bring to a boil again, lower heat and cook for 7–8 minutes, skimming off foam. Add *tofu*, Chinese cabbage and mushrooms, and when cabbage is tender, add *harusame* and leek. Add ingredients a bit at a time so as not to overcook, serving them as soon as they are cooked. Use *ponzu*, with *sarashi-negi* and *momiji-oroshi*, as dip. If *ponzu* is too strong, dilute with broth.

Notes

Do not overcook *harusame* and leek.

Variations

Use leftover soup by cooking rice or rice-cakes in it, with a thin layer of beaten egg over the top.

ちり鍋

CHIRI-NABÉ OF CHICKEN

MATSUMAE-NABÉ

THIS IS another dish originating in Hokkaido—in Matsu-mae, to be exact. Chicken is combined here with seafood, to the benefit of both.

Ingredients

1 lb. chicken fillet, sliced rather thin

4 prawns (2 oz. each), shelled (leaving tails intact), and deveined

½ lb. oysters (large), washed in lightly salted water, rinsed and drained

8 mushrooms (large), washed, stemmed and halved

3 stalks leek, cut into 2″ lengths

2 sheets *konbu*, cut into 6″ × 1″ rectangles, sponged on both sides with a damp cloth and slit lengthwise through center (prepare enough to cover bottom of skillet)

2 cups soup stock

Spices: *momiji-oroshi* (see basic recipe)

sarashi-negi (see basic recipe)

Ponzu sauce (see basic recipe)

Method

Spread *konbu* in skillet, arrange ingredients (except oysters) over *konbu*, add soup stock to ⅓ the depth of the ingredients and cook over high flame. Slip in oysters from the edge of the skillet, and when swelled, turn over and cook 1–2 minutes. When stock boils briskly, lower heat. When prawns change color, turn over and cook another 5–6 minutes. Chicken is done when it turns thoroughly white. Serve and eat while hot, dipping in *ponzu* with a pinch of the spices.

Notes

Do not overcook oysters. When broth cooks away during the cooking process, add more soup stock.

松前鍋

MATSUMAE-NABÉ
53

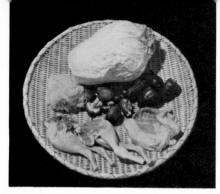 

CHICKEN MOONSTONE NABÉ (Tori Age-nabé)

CHICKEN, deep fried and then simmered in stock, has an intriguing new taste and texture.

Ingredients

2 lbs. chicken (with bones), cut into 2″ pieces, floured, allowed to stand for 1–2 minutes, and then deep fried until crisp in oil at 330°–340° F.

1 head Chinese cabbage (about 2 lbs.), sliced into 1½″ widths

¾ lb. *shirataki*, sectioned, boiled and drained

8 mushrooms, stemmed. Halve large ones.

4 bell peppers, stemmed, cut into quarters vertically, and seeded

Soup stock: 1 oz. dried bonito shavings, boiled with 4 cups water, 1 cup *mirin*, 1 cup soy sauce and 2 Tbsps. sugar for 4–5 minutes over low heat. Strain.

Method

Bring soup stock to a boil in a casserole, add chicken, Chinese cabbage, *shirataki* and mushrooms, and remove casserole to the hibachi on the table. When Chinese cabbage is tender, serve and eat with a sprinkling of 7-flavors pepper or red pepper.

Notes

The chicken is best when deep fried at the relatively low temperature given, allowing a little more time for it to cook thoroughly. For the best flavor, add it to the soup while it is still hot from the deep frying.

Variations

Tofu or leek may be added.

あげ鍋

**CHICKEN MOONSTONE
NABÉ
(Tori Age-nabé)**

TEN-DAY BANQUET NABÉ (Chanko-nabé)

THIS DISH has acquired fame as the customary diet of *sumo* wrestlers, whose tournaments traditionally were held on ten sunny days. Their enormous weight, however, cannot be attributed to this delicious dish itself, but to the great quantities consumed—accompanied by equally great quantities of rice. Try it and you will see why they never tire of it.

Ingredients

1 whole chicken, boned and sliced. Clean bones, pour boiling water over them, and cut into sections. Place bones in a pot with 10 cups of water, bring to a boil, and simmer for an hour over low heat (reduces to ¾ of its original volume). Skim foam from the top. Add 1 cup soy sauce, ⅓ cup *mirin*, 4 Tbsps. sugar, and cook further to reduce by 10%. Strain.

8 mushrooms, cleaned and stemmed

1 loaf *tofu*, soaked in water and then diced into 1″ cubes just prior to use

½ lb. *shirataki*

½ lb. bamboo shoot (boiled), cut into thin strips

1 carrot, cut diagonally while turning, and parboiled

1 head Chinese cabbage (2 lbs.), cut into 2″ widths. Halve large leaves.

1 lemon, cut into quarters

3 stalks leek, cut into 2″ lengths

Method

Fill casserole ⅔ full with soup stock, bring to boil, add chicken fillet and simmer for 2–3 minutes. Add Chinese cabbage, mushrooms, carrot, *shirataki*, *tofu* and leek, and cook for another 3 minutes. Remove foam from broth. Serve food with broth and eat, squeezing a little lemon juice over it if desired.

Notes

Add greens according to taste, and do not overcook. Use a large earthenware pot—or, if unavailable, use a deep skillet.

Variations

Lightly parboiled *daikon* or turnip can be added. Pork may be substituted for chicken.

ちゃんこ鍋

TEN-DAY BANQUET NABÉ (Chanko-nabé)

FALLING LEAF CHICKEN NABÉ
(Tsumiire-nabé)

GROUND CHICKEN, rarely utilized in Western cooking, has many applications in the Orient. This recipe, combining it with bean paste, gives chicken an interesting new taste and texture.

Ingredients

1 lb. ground chicken; 2 Tbsps. cornstarch; 1 Tbsp. red bean paste; 1 egg. Seasoning: 1 tsp. light soy sauce; 1 Tbsp. *mirin*; 1 Tbsp. soup stock.

Mix ground chicken with beaten egg, cornstarch, red bean paste and seasonings. Place mixture on a platter and flatten with a wet knife for ease in spooning it out uniformly.

1 head Chinese cabbage (2 lbs.). Parboil (see basic recipe), cool, spread on bamboo mat for cooking use *(makisu)*, alternating cabbage tops and ends to make uniform layer (see process illustration, page 101; a cloth can be used instead of bamboo), roll tightly, drain, and cut into 2″ slices.

1½ loaves *tofu*, diced into 1″ cubes

3 stalks leek cut into 2″ lengths

6 cups soup stock

Seasoning: 4 Tbsps. *mirin*; 6 Tbsps, soy sauce; 3 Tbsps. *saké*

2 lemons, quartered

Method

Pour soup stock into casserole with seasoning, bring to a boil and lower heat. Slide half of the chicken, by spoonfuls, into the soup and cook. Skim off foam and floating fat, add *tofu*, leek, and Chinese cabbage. Serve and eat with the soup, squeezing lemon juice over the top.

Notes

Do not boil soup over high heat. As the first ingredients are served, add the remaining chicken and vegetables, eating them as soon as they are cooked.

Variations

Round cabbage may be used instead of Chinese cabbage, and mushrooms, parboiled carrot, and greens such as *shungiku* and trefoil may be added. Grated *daikon* may be used as a spice.

つみ入れ鍋

**FALLING LEAF CHICKEN
NABÉ**

(Tsumiire-nabé)

CHICKEN NUGGET NABÉ (Tori Dango-nabé)

THIS FEATURES ground chicken, formed into balls and deep fried until crisp before being added, with vegetables, to a seasoned soup stock—and the result is delicious!

Ingredients

1 lb. ground chicken; $\frac{1}{2}$ oz. ginger root, grated; 1 egg; 2 Tbsps. flour. Seasoning: $\frac{1}{4}$ tsp. salt; 1 Tbsp. soy sauce. 1 Tbsp. saké; oil for deep frying.

Mix ground chicken with ginger juice, beaten egg, flour and seasoning. Squeeze mixture (see basic recipe) into a teaspoon, forming bite-sized balls, and deep fry in oil at 340° until brown.

1 carrot, parboiled, sliced $1\frac{1}{2}''$ thick and cut into plum-flower shapes

1 head Chinese cabbage (2 lbs.). Separate leaves and cut into $1\frac{1}{2}''$ widths, keeping hard lower sections separate from tender tops. Halve lengthwise, if large.

4 mushrooms (large), washed, stemmed and halved

6 cups soup stock

Seasoning: $\frac{1}{2}$ tsp. salt; $\frac{1}{3}$ cup light soy sauce; 3 Tbsps. *mirin*

Spices: 7-flavors pepper; prepared mustard

Method

Bring soup to boil, season, and put in some of the chicken balls, carrot, lower sections of Chinese cabbage, and cook until tender. Add a quantity of the cabbage tops and mushrooms and start serving, with some of the soup, as soon as these are tender. Add more as these are cooked and served.

Notes

Keep the oil temperature constant so that the chicken balls will be fried crisp to the core.

とり団子鍋

**CHICKEN NUGGET
NABÉ
(Tori Dango-nabé)**

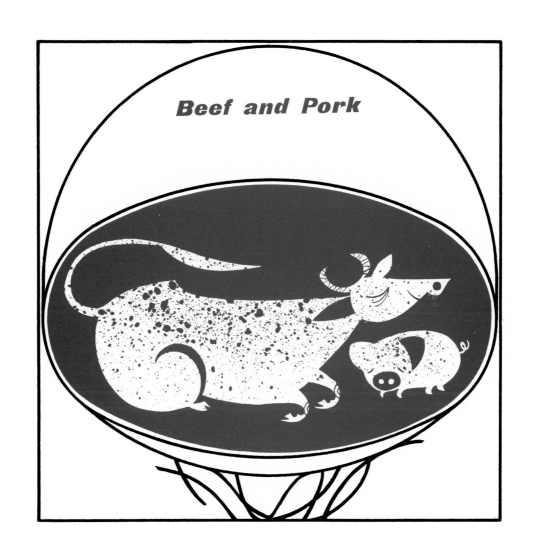

Beef and Pork

MEAT GRILL (Yakiniku)

THE SAUCE is the secret of this delectable beef, eaten with crisp, raw vegetables. It is readily adaptable to outdoor cooking, too.

Ingredients

1½ lbs. beef (rib roast or tenderloin), sliced into ¼″ thicknesses

Uncooked vegetables:

4 stalks (slender) celery, strung and soaked until crisp in ice water

½ head cabbage, cored and cut into 1½″ squares

2 small onions, sliced thin, separated into rings and crisped in ice water

2 bell peppers, stemmed, seeded, sliced into thin rings and crisped in ice water

Prior to use, drain vegetables and arrange in a bowl.

Sauce:

1 dried red pepper, seeded and chopped

2 tsps. white sesame seeds, parched with salt

1 stalk leek (slender), chopped

1 Tbsp. red bean paste

1 clove garlic, minced

Grind sesame seed with a pestle until oily, combine with other ingredients and mix well.

Method

Dredge meat with 2 Tbsps. of the sauce. Heat skillet and cook meat over high heat until just done to taste. Eat with remaining sauce and raw vegetables. (If you like, use your favorite salad dressing on the vegetables.)

Notes

Do not overcook meat. Dredge with sauce for only a short time before cooking or the meat flavor will be overpowered instead of enhanced. The sauce should be prepared just before use or the flavor will change.

Variations

Mutton or pork may be used in place of beef.

焼
肉

MEAT GRILL (Yakiniku)
65

PORK NABÉ (Buta-nabé)

THIN SLICES of pork harmonize with Chinese cabbage and a variety of ingredients in a zesty sauce.

Ingredients

  1 lb. sliced pork

  2 lbs. Chinese cabbage, halved lengthwise and sliced

  1 carrot, cut into strips and parboiled

  4 pieces *abura-age* (fried *tofu*), rinsed with boiling water and divided into strips

12   pieces roasted *fu*, soaked in water to soften and squeezed to remove excess water

  2 stalks leek, cut into 2″ lengths

  6 cups soup stock, seasoned with 4 Tbsps. soy sauce, 1 Tbsp. *mirin*, 2 tsps. salt, 1 Tbsp. *saké*, and $\frac{1}{2}$ tsp. monosodium glutamate

Method

  Fill casserole with seasoned soup stock, and vegetables, pork, and *abura-age*, and simmer until tender. Add roasted *fu* and simmer for 1–2 minutes. Serve with some of the soup. If you like, sprinkle with 7-flavors pepper.

Variations

  Use chicken meatballs or tuna instead of pork. Mushrooms may be added if desired. Chicken soup stock or ready-made soup base may be used instead of soup stock.

豚
鍋

PORK NABÉ (Buta-nabé)
67

SUKIYAKI

It PAYS to be patient when eating *sukiyaki*, the best known of all Japanese dishes, for the flavor increases with each succeeding round.

Ingredients

    1½ lbs. thinly sliced beef (sirloin or rib roast)

    2 loaves *tofu*, cut into 1″ cubes

    ¼ lb. *shirataki*, cut into 1″ lengths, boiled 1 minute and drained

    4 stalks leek, cut into 2″ lengths

    1 stick of *fu*, sliced 1″ thick, soaked in water to soften and pressed to drain

    2 bunches trefoil, cut into 2″ lengths

Arrange above ingredients attractively on a large platter.

    4 eggs (one per person), beaten in individual bowls

    Sauce: Equal parts of soy sauce, *mirin*, and sugar to taste

Method

    Oil preheated skillet thoroughly with suet or fat. Cover skillet with a single layer (not overlapping) of beef and sauté until well browned on both sides. This beef will not be especially tasty itself, but it gives a good flavor to the vegetables and beef to follow. Add some of the vegetables, *shirataki*, and *tofu* with a little of the sauce. Since the vegetables and *tofu* will give off liquid as they are cooked, add *saké*, soup stock, or more sauce instead of water as the broth reduces. Serve and eat, dipping the food into the beaten egg, and add more ingredients as the first batch is eaten.

Notes

The beef is best when sliced as thin as possible. This is easier to accomplish if the meat is partially frozen—or, ask your butcher to slice it for you. Turn the ingredients only once and do not overcook.

Variations

Dried mushrooms (softened in warm water), sliced fresh mushrooms, or watercress may be added. In Japan, it is popular to finish the meal with noodles or rice-cakes cooked in the leftover *sukiyaki* broth—or the thick broth may be poured over hot rice. Both are delicious!

すきやき

SUKIYAKI

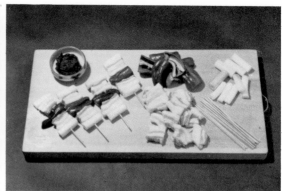

SKEWERED PORK NABÉ (Kushisashi-nabé)

PORK, leek, and green pepper are skewered together, sautéed, and then simmered in a highly seasoned stock.

Ingredients

    1 lb. fresh (uncured) pork bacon, cut into 1½″ squares, ½″ thick

    4 bell peppers (large), stemmed, quartered and seeded

    3 stalks leek, cut into 1½″ lengths

    Spear leek, pork and pepper on skewers in that order. Roll in flour, sauté in 2 Tbsps. oil until brown on both sides.

    2 cups soup stock, seasoned with 1 Tbsp. red bean paste (blend first with a little stock), ¼ cup *mirin*, ¼ cup soy sauce and 2 Tbsps. sugar.

Method

    Bring seasoned stock to a boil, lower heat, add the sautéed, skewered ingredients, and cook for 2–3 minutes over medium heat. Turn and cook the other side for 1–2 minutes. Remove to bowls, serve and eat, sprinkling with 7-flavors pepper.

Notes

    If pork is thicker than ½″, pepper and leek will be overcooked before the pork is done.

Variations

    Chicken fillet may be substituted for pork, and onion for leek. Use beaten egg as dip, and powdered *sansho* instead of 7-flavors pepper.

串さし鍋

SKEWERED PORK NABÉ (Kushisashi-nabé)

GOLDEN CLOUD NABÉ (Kawari-yanagawa-nabé)

Here the ingredients are all cooked—but in a prescribed order—before serving begins. The dish is topped with a thin layer of beaten egg.

Ingredients

½ lb. pork, sliced thin and cut into 1″ widths
1 lb. bean sprouts, ends cut, washed and drained
1 loaf *konnyaku* (½ lb.), rubbed well with salt, washed, shredded and roasted in a dry skillet
1 oz. string beans, strung, boiled with a pinch of salt, rinsed in cold water. Shred diagonally.
1 piece ginger root, peeled and shredded
3 eggs, well beaten
4 cups soup stock
Seasoning: 5 Tbsps. sugar; 2 Tbsps. *mirin*; 6 Tbsps. light soy sauce

Method

Put soup stock in casserole, add *konnyaku*, sugar and *mirin*, and cook for 2–3 minutes. Sprinkle shredded ginger over all and flavor with soy sauce. Add bean sprouts and pork, and cook another 2–3 minutes over medium heat. Skim off foam. Sprinkle shredded beans over the top and pour the beaten egg in a thin layer over them. Cook for 3–4 minutes or until the egg is partially done. Remove a portion to each platter and serve with 7-flavors pepper.

Notes

A skillet may be used in place of the casserole.

Variations

Chicken meatballs may be used instead of pork, and mushrooms may be added.

変り柳川鍋

GOLDEN CLOUD NABÉ (Kawari-yanagawa-nabé)

73

SHABU-SHABU

THIS IS a great party dish—and your guests will enjoy participating in the cooking. The name, *shabu-shabu* (pronounced shah-bu), comes from the sound made by swishing the ingredients back and forth in the bubbling broth.

Ingredients
- 1½ lbs. beef (rib roast or tenderloin), sliced very thin (Partially frozen meat is easier to slice.)
- 1½ loaves *tofu* (1 lb.), cut into 1″ cubes
- 8 mushrooms, cleaned and stemmed. Halve large ones.
- ½ lb. *shirataki*, cut into 2″ lengths and parboiled
- ½ head Chinese cabbage. Steam cabbage in one cup boiling water in tightly covered pan. Drain, sprinkle with salt, and cool.
- ½ lb. spinach. Wash well and steam in ½ cup water, rinse in cold water, straighten and drain. Roll with cabbage (see basic recipe).
- 1 bunch trefoil, roots discarded, cut into 2″ lengths

Arrange above ingredients attractively on a platter.
- 1 sheet *konbu* (4″ square), sponged and slit across fibers
- Spices: *sarashi-negi* (see basic recipe)
          momiji-oroshi (see basic recipe)
- *Ponzu* sauce (see basic recipe)

Sesame sauce: ½ cup white sesame seed; 3 Tbsps. soup stock; 2 Tbsps. vinegar; 1½ Tbsps. light soy sauce; 1 Tbsp. *mirin*; ½ tsp. monosodium glutamate. Parch sesame seeds with a little salt in a dry skillet and then grind with a pestle until oily. Add soup stock, vinegar, soy sauce and *mirin*, a little at a time, while continuing to grind. Add monosodium glutamate.

Method
Fill a large casserole or a large, heavy skillet ¾ full of water, add *konbu*, bring to a boil and remove *konbu*. Holding beef with chopsticks, swish in boiling soup stock for about half a minute. Dip hot meat in sesame or *ponzu* sauce, to which the desired spice has been added, and eat. Other ingredients are cooked in the same manner until just done. Those that take a little longer to cook may be dropped in and retrieved with chopsticks when done.

Notes
The meat should be sliced as thin as possible. Skim foam from broth as it forms. Soup stock should be boiling briskly when ingredients are added.

しゃぶしゃぶ

SHABU-SHABU

JINGISUKAN-NABÉ

Perhaps you will recognize this as "Genghis-Khan." It is prepared on a special dome-shaped grill, and this dish, too, can be prepared out-of-doors or at the table. Either way, it will score highly with family and guests.

Ingredients
- 1½ lbs. mutton or beef (sirloin or tenderloin), sliced thin
- 2 oz. suet or fat
- 2 onions, sliced ¼″ thick
- 1 lemon, quartered
- 8 mushrooms, stemmed
- 2 stalks leek, cut into 2″ lengths
- Spices: *momiji-oroshi* (see basic recipe)
  - 1 oz. ginger root, peeled and grated
  - 2 cloves garlic, chopped and frizzled in 1 Tbsp. oil
  - 1 onion, grated
  - 2 slender stalks leek, chopped

Place spices in separate small bowls.
Sauce: Mix ½ cup soy sauce, ½ cup pressed apple juice, ¼ cup *mirin*, 2 Tbsps. wine or *saké*, and ½ tsp. monosodium glutamate.

Method
Heat *jingisukan* pan, place suet in the middle until the oil melts over the dome, and arrange meat and vegetables on dome. When meat changes color a little, turn over and cook to taste. Eat, dipping in sauce with the spices of your choice—or sprinkle with lemon juice.

Notes
Preheat pan over high heat and lower to medium before starting to cook. The ratio of ingredients for the sauce may be changed according to taste. Flavor the sauce with lemon juice or 7-flavors pepper if you like.

Variations
The meat may be marinated in the sauce for 20 minutes prior to cooking.

ジンギスカン鍋

JINGISUKAN-NABÉ

77

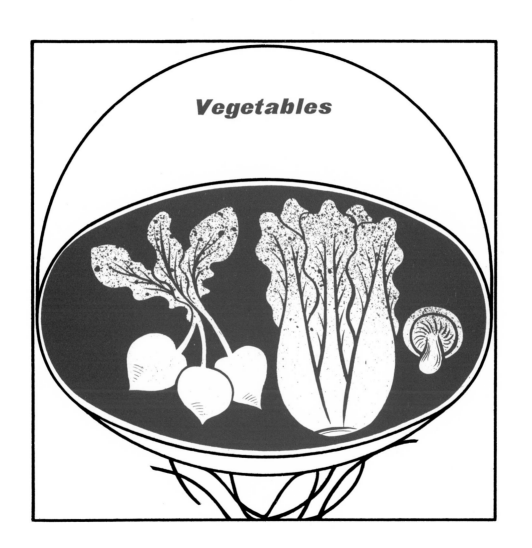

NOODLE SUKIYAKI (Udon-suki)

AN INTERESTING combination—clams and chicken—cooked in a flavorful broth with vegetables and homemade noodles.

Ingredients

Homemade noodles for 4 (see basic recipe)

Drop noodles into rapidly boiling water, stirring slowly to separate. When water comes to a boil again, add a cup of cold water. Bring to a boil again and cook for 3–4 minutes. Pour noodles into a colander and rinse under cold running water until cool, rubbing gently with hands to remove excess starch, and drain.

$\frac{1}{2}$ lb. chicken fillet, sliced thin

8 clams (medium), soaked in salt water (2 Tbsps. salt per 5 cups of water) barely to cover, for 5–6 hours. Wash in fresh water to remove slippery coating from shells. Cut ligaments (see process illustration).

8 mushrooms, cleaned, stemmed and halved, if large

1 small head Chinese cabbage (2 lbs.)

$\frac{1}{2}$ lb. spinach. Parboil cabbage and spinach, and roll (see process illustrations, page 101). Cut into 1″ slices.

1 lemon, quartered

12 small pieces roasted *fu*, soaked in water to soften and pressed to drain

5 cups soup stock, seasoned with $\frac{1}{2}$ cup soy sauce, $\frac{1}{4}$ cup *mirin*, 3 Tbsps. sugar, and 1 tsp. monosodium glutamate.

Method

Pour $\frac{2}{3}$ of the seasoned soup stock into casserole and bring to a boil. Add part of the noodles, chicken, clams, mushrooms, Chinese cabbage, etc., and cook for 5–6 minutes over medium heat. Serve food with a little of the broth, and sprinkle with lemon juice. Add soup as needed to cook the remaining ingredients.

Notes

The soup stock may appear mildly seasoned at the start, but it will reduce as it cooks and the ingredients will add to the flavor. Seasonings for the soup stock may be adjusted to taste. Prepare seasoned soup stock in quantity when there are to be many diners, and add to the casserole gradually while cooking.

Variations

Spaghetti, macaroni, or other noodles may be used.

うどんすき

NOODLE SUKIYAKI (Udon-suki)

81

BUBBLING TOFU (Yudofu)

Yudofu is a *tofu* dish prepared by boiling. This is an especially good variation combining shrimp and chicken.

Ingredients

2 loaves *tofu*, soaked in cold water, then diced into 1″ cubes just prior to cooking

4 mushrooms, cleaned and stemmed

½ lb. chicken fillet, cut into 1″ pieces

8 shrimps, shelled (leaving tails intact), deveined

6″ square sheet of *konbu*, slit across fibers several times

Spices: 2 stalks leek, chopped and placed in small bowl; 1 oz. ginger root, peeled and grated into a small bowl

Sauce for dip: ⅔ cup soy sauce; ⅓ cup water; ⅓ cup *mirin;* ½ oz. dried bonito shavings; 4″ square sheet *konbu*. Combine ingredients in a pot and bring to a boil over low heat; strain through a cloth.

Method

Put *konbu* in an earthenware pot with 3–4 cups water and bring to a boil. Add chicken and shrimp, and cook for 2–3 minutes over medium heat. Skim off foam. Add *tofu* and mushrooms, and bring to a boil again. Add a pinch of leek and ginger to sauce, and dip food before eating.

Notes

Be careful not to cook over high flame— *tofu* hardens and develops holes when overcooked. The dip will be less flavorful when cool. Keep it warm by placing it in a small cup in the center of the casserole.

Variations

Pork or shellfish (shells removed) may be used instead of chicken. Parboiled cauliflower may be added.

湯豆腐

BUBBLING TOFU (Yudofu)

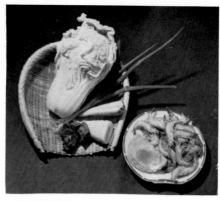

TEMPLE OF JADE NABÉ (Hakusai-nabé)

SHRIMP AND ham give a tantalizing flavor to Chinese cabbage in this *nabé-mono*.

Ingredients

1 small head of Chinese cabbage (2 lbs.), cut into $1\frac{1}{2}''$ chunks

4 large dried mushrooms, soaked in warm water to soften, stemmed and cut into thirds

$\frac{1}{2}$ lb. bamboo shoot (boiled), cut into $1\frac{1}{2}''$ lengths and sliced into thin strips

2 stalks leek, cut into diagonal sections

$\frac{1}{2}$ carrot, sliced thin, halved and parboiled

1 lb. shrimp, washed in lightly salted water, shelled, heads and black veins removed

4 thin slices boiled ham, quartered

5 cups soup stock, seasoned with 1 tsp. salt, 1 Tbsp. light soy sauce and 2 Tbsps. *mirin*

Method

Place a portion of each ingredient except green leek in a casserole with the seasoned soup stock, bring to a boil, lower heat and cook for 4–5 minutes or until cabbage is tender. Skim off foam while simmering. Add leek last. Serve with some of the broth, adding more ingredients to replace those served. A squeeze of lemon juice or a little 7-flavors pepper may be added to taste.

Notes

Be careful to remove foam and scum thoroughly.

Variations

Chicken or meatballs may be used instead of boiled ham and shrimp. Fresh mushrooms may be used.

白菜鍋

TEMPLE OF JADE NABÉ (Hakusai-nabé)

85

SUNFLOWER NABÉ (Daikon Soboro-nabé)

DAIKON, the giant white radish of Japan, is the star of this dish. It may be found in Japanese or Chinese food stores in the larger cities, but turnip makes a more than satisfactory substitute.

Ingredients

1 *daikon* (2 lbs.), washed and cubed (cut while turning). Boil until tender in water to cover, with a pinch of rice to keep it white.

1 carrot ($\frac{1}{2}$ lb.), sliced and parboiled

$\frac{1}{2}$ onion (3 oz.), diced

1 large tomato, cored. Holding tomato with a fork, dip it into boiling water for 30–40 seconds. Rinse in ice water, peel, slice thin, remove seeds, and dice.

4 dried mushrooms, soaked in warm water, stemmed and diced

11 oz. ground pork

5 cups soup stock

2 Tbsps. vegetable oil

Seasoning: 5 Tbsps. soy sauce; 2 Tbsps. *mirin;* 2 Tbsps. sugar

7-flavors pepper

Method

Heat oil and sauté ground pork, stirring often, until brown. Add mushrooms, onion and tomato, and sauté quickly. Pour soup stock into casserole, add *daikon* and carrot, and simmer for 10 minutes over low heat, removing foam from the top. Add seasoning (above) and cook for 20 minutes over low heat. Bring casserole to the table and serve, sprinkling with 7-flavors pepper or white pepper.

Variations

Substitute turnip for *daikon*, and add sliced celery to increase the flavor. Ground chicken may be used in place of pork, and fresh mushrooms in place of dried mushrooms.

そぼろ鍋

SUNFLOWER NABÉ (Daikon Soboro-nabé)

SKEWERED HOTCHPOTCH (Miso Oden)

YET ANOTHER dish proving the versatility of bean paste.

Ingredients

1 *daikon* (2 lbs.), sliced ½″ thick, peeled, sharp edges trimmed (see basic recipe). Halve slices, if large. Parboil in water to cover, with 1 tsp. rice to whiten, and spear each piece with a bamboo skewer.

1 loaf *tofu*. Cut in strips 3″ × 1″ × ½″ and spear each with 2 skewers.

2 loaves *konnyaku* (1 lb.), rubbed well with salt, lightly pounded with wooden pestle, cleaned, cut in strips 2 × ½″ and skewered

6″ square sheet *konbu*, sponged, and slit through fibers (not to edges)

neri-miso (mixed bean paste): 5 oz. ground chicken; 1 pc. ginger root (peeled); 3 oz. red bean paste; 4 oz. white bean paste; 2/3 cup soup stock; 1 Tbsp. oil; and seasoning. Sauté ground chicken and ginger in oil, mixing well. Add red bean paste, white bean paste, 2 Tbsps. sugar, 3 Tbsps. *mirin*, and soup stock. Lower heat and simmer for 10–15 minutes, stirring well to form a paste.

Method

Put *konbu* in casserole, with the *neri-miso* in a slender cup in the center. Arrange skewered *tofu*, *konnyaku* and *daikon* around the cup, add water barely to cover, and bring to a boil over medium heat. Remove casserole to hibachi on the table, dip skewered ingredients into the *neri-miso* and serve. Add 7-flavors pepper or powdered *sansho* according to taste.

Notes

Soak *tofu* in water until used, and do not overcook it or it will harden.

Variations

Ground pork may be substituted for ground chicken in the bean paste. Oysters, sliced pork or chicken fillet may be skewered and added to the ingredients, using sesame seed sauce instead of bean paste. Parboiled turnip may replace *daikon*, and parboiled cauliflower is a good addition.

みそおでん

SKEWERED HOTCHPOTCH
(Miso Oden)

TOKYO HOTCHPOTCH (Oden)

This dish originated in the area centered around Tokyo. Bite-sized balls of ground beef and pork are deep fried and then simmered for a long time with the other ingredients in well-seasoned stock.

Ingredients

1 *daikon* ($\frac{1}{4}$ lb.), sliced 1″ thick, peeled, sharp edges trimmed (see basic recipe). Boil in water to cover with 1 tsp. rice (to whiten) until it can be pierced by a bamboo skewer.

4 medium potatoes (1$\frac{1}{2}$ lb.), parboiled in water to cover and peeled while hot

1 loaf *tofu*, diced into 1″ cubes

1$\frac{1}{2}$ loaves *konnyaku* ($\frac{3}{4}$ lb.), rubbed with salt, lightly pounded, cleaned and cut into triangles

8 loaves *atsu-age*, rinsed well by pouring boiling water over them

Meatballs: $\frac{3}{4}$ lb. mixed ground beef and pork; $\frac{1}{2}$ onion; 1 beaten egg; 2 Tbsps. flour. Mix ingredients and season with $\frac{2}{3}$ tsp. salt and $\frac{1}{4}$ tsp. monosodium glutamate. Form into bite-sized balls and deep fry until crisp in 340°–360° F. oil for 4–5 minutes.

Spice: 2 Tbsps. mustard

8 cups soup stock

Seasoning: 3 Tbsps. sugar; 7 Tbsps. light soy sauce; 3 Tbsps. *mirin*

Method

Put soup and seasoning in a large casserole, add all ingredients except *tofu*, and bring to a boil over high heat. Lower heat so that the broth moves only slightly, and cook for 3 hours. Add *tofu* 30 minutes before serving time.

Notes

The secret is in cooking the ingredients in thin soup for a long time over low heat. When many vegetables are used, dried bonito shavings (in a cheesecloth bag) may be added for additional flavor.

お
で
ん

TOKYO HOTCHPOTCH (Oden)
91

MENU FOR NABÉ-MONO DINNERS

Since one of these dishes contains as great a variety of ingredients as a conventional dinner, very little else is required. However, for the sake of contrast to the hot dish, a cold, piquant side dish should be included. *Suno-mono* (a vinegared vegetable such as cucumber), *hitashi* (cold, boiled greens), *goma-ae* (greens with sesame sauce), or *shiro-ae* (greens coated with bean curd) are good complementary dishes. Assorted Japanese pickles go extremely well with *nabé-mono*. With soupless casseroles, such as *sukiyaki* or *teppan-yaki*, prepare *osumashi* (clear) or *miso* soup. Rice, if you like, followed by dessert and tea, will complete a most satisfying meal.

Clear Soup

A DELICATE clear soup that is a delight to the eye as well as the palate.

Ingredients

4 pieces (1 oz. each) sea bream or any white meat fish fillet (flounder, whitefish, etc.). Cut each piece into 2 sections, simmer for 3 minutes in boiling salt water (1 tsp. salt per 3 cups water).

1½″ length of *udo*, peeled, cut into thin strips, and rinsed in water.

1½ oz. trefoil or *shungiku*. Parboil briefly to heighten color, drain, and cut into 1½″ lengths.

4 *sansho* leaves, or peel of fresh citron

4 cups soup stock, seasoned with 1 tsp. salt and 1–2 drops soy sauce.

Method

Arrange 2 pieces of sea bream, *udo* and trefoil in a bowl and gently pour the hot soup over them. Float the *sansho* leaf or citron peel on top.

Notes

If boiled sea bream has been allowed to cool, warm in another pan with a small quantity of stock before serving.

Variations

Wedged citron or lemon may be used instead of *sansho* leaves for flavoring.

Soup stock for suimono

Ingredients

4″ square sheet *konbu*, both sides sponged with damp cloth, slits made across fibers

½ to 1 oz. dried bonito, preferably shaved just prior to use

Method

Heat 5 cups of water with the *konbu*, lower heat and

remove *konbu* just before the boiling point is reached and add the dried bonito shavings; turn off heat and let stand until shavings settle and then strain through a cloth (or several layers of cheesecloth).

Notes

Boiling *konbu* and dried bonito shavings rapidly over high heat will not make a good soup stock.

Akadashi

RED BEAN paste lends its inimitable flavor to sea bream in this savory soup.

Ingredients

11 oz. sea bream (with bone). Cut into 1½″ sections, place in boiling water for a short time, take out and submerge in cold water, wash thoroughly, and scale.

4″ square sheet of *konbu*, prepared as in previous recipe

¼ sheet *fu* (thin strip). Wrap in wet cloth to moisten, divide and place in bowls.

½ oz. trefoil, chopped

2 oz. red bean paste

Sansho

Method

Boil 5 cups water and add the *konbu* and prepared sea bream (over medium heat). Lower heat and remove *konbu* just before the boiling point is reached, and simmer for 10 minutes over low heat. Skim off foam and floating fat thoroughly. Dissolve red bean paste in a small quantity of the soup and add this mixture to the soup. Check the flavor and add soy sauce to taste. Pour soup into the bowls, sprinkle with chopped trefoil and powdered *sansho*.

Notes

When making delicate fish soup, be careful not to boil the fish over high heat. It should be simmered slowly.

Variations

Any white meat fish fillet (sea bass, flounder, etc.) will do if it is fresh.

Sunomono

BOILED HAM and cucumber, served well chilled with a tart sauce.

Ingredients

1 cucumber (5 oz.). Roll on a board with salt to brighten green color. Halve lengthwise and slice diagonally.

2 slices boiled ham, cut into 1½×¼″ strips

½ oz. ginger root. Grate, and mix juice with ¼ cup *sanbai-zu*.

Method

Chill ingredients. Just before serving pour sauce over ingredients and stir together.

Notes

If sauce is combined with the ingredients in advance, juice will form and the flavor and color will be lost. Serve *sunomono* on small individual plates, shaping into a tiny pile and topping with shredded red pickled ginger, fine dried bonito shavings, or shredded and rinsed ginger root.

Variations

Instead of cucumber, sliced cold boiled cabbage or lightly boiled bean sprouts may be used. Pickled cucumber or tiny pickled onions may be applied as garnish.

Shiro-ae

THE WHITE sauce that is the basis for this taste-teasing dish bears no relationship to the white sauce of the West. Your guests will try in vain to guess its ingredients.

Ingredients

4 oz. *daikon*, $\frac{1}{4}$ carrot (1$\frac{1}{2}$ oz.). Shred both, rub until soft with salt, wash in water and squeeze out excess moisture.

3 dried mushrooms. Soak in lukewarm water to soften. Stem and shred. Simmer with 2 tsps. soy sauce, 1 tsp. *mirin* over low heat and let cool.

$\frac{1}{2}$ loaf *konnyaku* (4 oz.). Rub well with salt, wash, beat with wooden pestle, and shred. Fry in a dry skillet and let cool.

$\frac{2}{3}$ loaf *tofu* (7 oz.). Wrap in a dry cloth, place a chopping block or weight on top, and let stand for 10 minutes to drain.

1 Tbsp. white sesame seeds, 1$\frac{1}{2}$ oz. white bean paste. Roast sesame seeds with a little salt in a dry skillet, grind well with a pestle until oily. Break up the *tofu* and mix it well with the white bean paste and ground sesame seeds. Season with 1 Tbsp. *mirin* and 1 tsp. sugar.

Method

Combine *tofu* mixture with *daikon*, carrot, mushroom and *konnyaku*. Serve in small bowls in the shape of a little mountain.

Notes

Combine just before serving. Keep *tofu* in fresh water under refrigeration until used, especially in hot weather. Drain as directed above.

Variations

Konnyaku may be omitted.

Aemono

THIS SAUCE makes string beans something more than an "ordinary vegetable."

Ingredients

6 oz. string beans. String, boil in salt water (1 Tbsp. salt per 5 cups water) just until tender. Cool rapidly in cold water and drain.

1½ oz. roasted peanuts. Remove thin skins, chop and grind well. Mix with 1½ Tbsps. sugar, 2 Tbsps. soy sauce and ¼ tsp. monosodium glutamate.

Method

Cut string beans into 1½″ lengths, pile in a dish, cover with peanut sauce, top with dried bonito shavings and serve.

Notes

Cut string beans after boiling since it would make them juicy to boil after cutting. To make a smooth sauce, grind peanuts well before adding seasonings.

Variations

Roast 3 Tbsps. white sesame seeds, grind, season with 1½ Tbsps. sugar, 2 Tbsps. soy sauce and use as topping for boiled string beans.

Spinach Hitashi

Wash spinach and then parboil briefly. Drain and cut to 1¼″ size. Mix 1½ Tbsp. soy sauce with 1 Tbsp. soup stock or hot water, and dash of monosodium glutamate for sauce. Arrange boiled spinach on a plate, garnish with shredded dried bonito. Pour sauce on spinach to eat.

Basic Recipes

PONZU SAUCE

Combine ⅓ cup sour orange or lemon juice, ½ cup soy sauce and ⅓ cup soup stock. When used as dip for *nabé-mono*, broth from the dish may be used instead of soup stock. Add more of any ingredient to taste during the meal.

SANBAI-ZU

Mix ½ cup vinegar, 2 Tbsps. sugar, ½ tsp. soy sauce, ½ tsp. salt and a dash of monosodium glutamate. Use as a marinade for *sunomono*, etc.

TEMPURA BATTER

1½ cups flour; cold water to make one cup when added to 1 eaten egg. Sift flour and mix with water and egg.

TEMPURA SAUCE

Combine 1 cup water, ½ cup each of soy sauce, *mirin*, dried bonito shavings, and bring to a boil. Remove from heat, add a dash of monosodium glutamate and then strain. Cool and use as a dip for *tempura*.

SOUP STOCK FOR NABÉ-MONO (6 (6 CUPS)

4″ square sheet *konbu*, sponged on both sides with a damp cloth and slit several times across fibers; ½ oz. dried bonito shavings. Combine *konbu* and dried bonito shavings with 7 cups of water in a pot and bring to a boil. Remove *konbu* just before boiling point is reached and simmer stock for 1–2 minutes over low heat. Remove from heat and strain through a cloth.

SOY SOUP

Bring ½ cup *mirin* to a boil, add ½ cup soy sauce, 1 cup water and ½ oz. dried bonito shavings, and bring to a boil again. Remove from heat, strain and cool.

PARBOILING OF SPINACH (AND OTHER GREENS)

Remove roots, clean thoroughly, and make slits through ends of stems to facilitate even cooking. Bring ½ cup water to boil in a kettle, add spinach, cover tightly and cook over medium heat. When steam seeps out, turn spinach, cover and continue to simmer for a short while. Remove spinach and cool quickly under cold water. Arrange spinach with stems in one direction and drain well. If a large quantity is being prepared, repeat the procedure 2 or 3 times, changing the water each time.

PARBOILING OF CHINESE CABBAGE (OR ROUND CABBAGE)

Core and separate leaves. Boil in 1 cup of water in tightly covered kettle over medium or low heat. Turn once and simmer until tender. Remove, sprinkle with salt to bring out the flavor, and drain well. When preparing a large quantity, repeat the process several times, adding more water when necessary. To prevent the cabbage from boiling dry and burning, cook over medium or low heat.

HAKATA OF CHINESE CABBAGE AND SPINACH

Spread leaves of Chinese cabbage, alternating tops with lower ends to make a uniform layer, in a square tin, folding over the ends if they are too long. Cover with a layer of boiled spinach. Repeat this process several times, press firmly to drain, turn tin upside down onto a board—emptying contents carefully—and cut into pieces of the desired size.

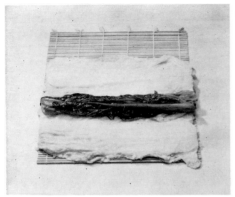 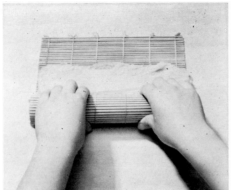 

CHINESE CABBAGE AND SPINACH ROLL

Beat the hard veins of parboiled Chinese cabbage with the back of a heavy cooking knife to soften (this facilitates rolling). Straighten parboiled spinach and drain well. Spread leaves of Chinese cabbage on a bamboo mat for kitchen use, alternating tops and ends. Place spinach on top in the same manner. Lift one edge of the mat with thumbs, press spinach with other fingers, roll tightly and drain. Form a uniform cylinder, unwrap mat, and cut as directed in recipe. (A thick cloth may be used in place of the bamboo mat.)

TRIMMING SHARP EDGES

To prevent square-cut or sliced *daikon*, turnip, carrot and potato from losing shape while cooking, trim off the edges while turning with the left hand.

"SQUEEZING" MEAT BALLS

Place 2 Tbsps. ground meat or chicken (seasoned according to recipe) in left hand, squeeze the mixture out between thumb and forefinger onto a teaspoon, shaping into bite-sized balls.

METHOD OF PREPARING CLAMS FOR COOKING

To prevent clam shells from opening and losing their flavorful juices while cooking, cut off ligaments prior to use. (Note: Choose live clams or shellfish whenever possible. These will crackle sharply when struck against each other. Others will produce a dull sound.)

ABURA-AGE

Tofu, cut $\frac{1}{2}''$ thick, drained on dry cloth for 4–5 minutes, and deep fried in oil at 330°–340°F. for 5–6 minutes. This is customarily used after removing the oil by pouring boiling water over it. *Atsu-age* is another variation—cut 1″ thick and deep fried longer.

FILLETING OF FISH

Choose fresh fish and prepare it for cooking soon after it is purchased—scaling, removing entrails and washing in water. If it is kept for any length of time without first

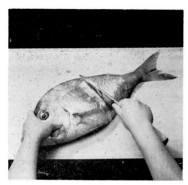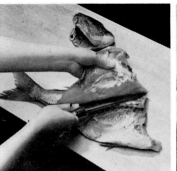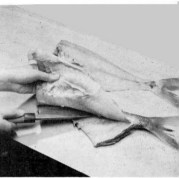

being cleaned, it will lose its freshness. If the surface is dry, soak in salted water for a while to facilitate scaling.

Method
(1) Holding the head of the fish with the left hand, scrape scales with a heavy kitchen knife, working from tail to head and tilting the back a little to the left (see process illustration). Work carefully around the head, back and tail.
(2) Slit the mandible crosswise and cut open the belly from the mandible down to the ventral fins. Remove entrails and gills, wash thoroughly and drain. This process is called *mizu-arai*—or cleaning up! ' To remove the head, thrust the edge of the knife straight down between head and body to the center bone (illustration); do other side in the same way, severing the bone.
(3) Separate flesh of underside horizontally from ven-

tral fin to the base of the tail along the center bone, freeing the small bones with the point of the knife. Sever the flesh above the center bone from head to tail (illustration). Do not use a sawing motion but work with repeated long strokes from head to tail.
(4) Put remaining half of fish on the cutting board, bone down, with the tail to your left. Make a slit at the base of the dorsal fin, and cut flesh above the bone from head to tail along the bone. Turn tail to the right side, and cut flesh from the underside, freeing small bones and separating flesh from the center bone.

Notes
White meat fish fillet, when called for in *nabé-mono*, refers to fillets from which all fine bones have been removed. Around 50% of the purchase weight may be used as fillet.

BOILING OF DRIED NOODLES

Bring ample water to a full boil in a large kettle and drop in noodles, separating with chopsticks or a fork. When water comes to a boil again, add $\frac{1}{2}$ cup cold water to stop the boiling. Repeat this process a second time. When water reaches a boil the third time, lower heat and simmer for 2–3 minutes. Remove from heat and place noodles in cold water to cool, rubbing gently with hands to remove excess starch, and drain.

An insufficient amount of water will thicken from the starch and hinder the boiling process. Failure to separate noodles immediately will cause them to stick together in "dumplings," but continuous stirring will tear the noodles.

HOMEMADE NOODLES

Ingredients (for 4)
1 lb. ($3\frac{3}{4}$–4 cups) hard flour
1 cup salt water (2 Tbsp. salt)

Method

Sift flour into a mound on a board, making a hollow in the center. Gradually pour in the salt water, mixing with your hand as you pour. Knead well into a soft dough. Let stand for 30 minutes, wrapped in a damp cloth.

Knead again firmly. Roll out the dough, pulling it as you wrap it around the rolling pin—stretching it a bit more each time. Continue to sprinkle it with flour each time you roll and stretch it to prevent it from sticking to the rolling pin. Repeat this process several times. Spread the dough out in a sheet $\frac{1}{8}''$–$\frac{1}{4}''$ thick, fold into pleats, and cut it into $\frac{1}{4}''$ strips. Separate strands.

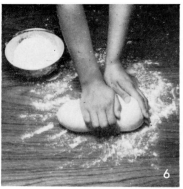

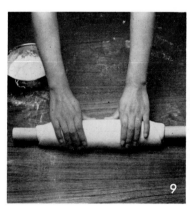

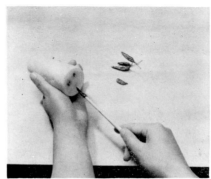

Spices and Dips

Spices and dips are an integral part of *nabé-mono*, enhancing the flavors and bringing out the best in the ingredients. A word about a few of these might be helpful. Some may be new to you and some may be old favorites, perhaps used in a new way.

(1) *Sarashi-negi* (chopped leek) is used in Japan in both casserole and noodle dishes. Cut white part of leek into 1½″ lengths, halve lengthwise, remove core, and shred lengthwise along fibers. Wrap in a cloth and immerse in cold water. Change water and let stand a few minutes and then drain well.

(2) Chopped leek may also be used without the water treatment. Its strong flavor enhances the flavor of the broth and may be preferred by some.

(3) Grated *daikon* is used with casserole dishes and *tempura*. Grate *daikon* (no need to peel) and drain. White radish could be used where *daikon* is unavailable.

(4) *Momiji-oroshi* is *daikon* with seeded, dried red peppers inserted into holes made in the cut end. This is then grated and drained of excess juice. (see photos above)

(5) Powdered *sansho* is used in Golden Cloud *Nabé*, Seafood *Sukiyaki*, and Skewered Hotchpotch. It may be added to the dish while cooking or sprinkled on to taste when served.

(6) 7-flavors pepper, a blend of seven different spices, is popular with noodle dishes and with *nabé-mono*. It comes in three strengths, hot, medium and mild, and has a delightfully different aroma. You might want to experiment with it in Western cookery.

(7) Mustard paste is prepared by pouring hot water, a few drops at a time, over dry mustard (Japanese or English is best) in a small cup, and stirring quickly with

chopsticks until a creamy paste is formed. Turn the cup upside down and let stand for 10–15 minutes. This is hot and should be used sparingly.

(8) Lemon. A little lemon juice heightens the flavor of those dishes cooked in a thin soup.

(9) Grated ginger root. This should be fresh ginger root and is usually available in those stores selling Oriental foodstuffs. Powdered ginger is *not* a good substitute and it would be better to omit it entirely. Bottled ginger juice could be used in a pinch.

(10) *Yuzu* is a type of citron, the peel of which does marvelous things to the flavor of a clear soup such as *suimono*. A bit of lemon or grapefruit rind can be substituted, but the effect is not the same.

(11) *Goma*, or sesame seeds, are usually roasted with salt in a dry skillet and then ground until oily, preferably, in a *suribachi*—a grinding bowl with a serrated interior—using a wooden pestle.

(12) *Katsuo-bushi* is dried bonito that is shaved, preferably just prior to use, and used in making soup stock.

(13) Egg. This might startle the uninitiated, but a raw egg, beaten with chopsticks in a small bowl, makes an excellent dip for *sukiyaki* and some of the other dishes. (Be sure to tell your guests that the egg is not cooked—or they might crack it as one would a hard-boiled egg—with dire results!) The morsel of hot food, taken directly from the simmering pot and dipped into the egg, 'cooks' the coating of egg that adheres to it—and the flavor is superb!

Glossary

abura-age: Fried, thin slices of *tofu* (*see* p. 102).

atsu-age: Fried, thick slices of *tofu* (*see* p. 102).

bonito shavings, dried (*katsuo-bushi*): *see* p. 107. A convenient combination of *konbu* and bonito shavings in "teabag" form for making soup stock is sometimes available under the name *Dashi-no-moto*.

Chinese cabbage: Round cabbage can be substituted, if necessary.

daikon: Giant white radish. Turnips can be substituted (*see* p. 106).

fu: A light "crouton" made of wheat gluten; used in *sukiyaki*, soups, and one-pot cookery.

ginger root: Fresh ginger is costly, but is usually available in the West, depending on the locality (*see* p. 107).

ginger, pickled red: An excellent garnish also for many occasions other than a Japanese repast.

ginko nuts: The succulent nuts of the ginko tree. These are not always available in the West.

green chili pepper: The small green chilis used in Japanese cooking are sweet and not hot. Bell pepper is an adequate substitute.

hakata rolls: *see* p. 100.

harusame: Clear vermicelli made from bean starch.

hitashi: *see* p. 96.

konbu: Dried kelp; used mostly as a soup stock base.

konnyaku: A stiff, jellylike cake made from devil's tongue starch.

makisu: A flexible bamboo mat, about the size of a place mat, used for shaping foods into rolls.

mirin: Sweet *saké* used for cooking. *Saké* sweetened with sugar to taste can be substituted, as can a sweet Western white wine.

miso: Bean paste; used for *miso* soup, flavorings and sauces. *Miso* comes in a spectrum of flavors and colors, from very salty to "sweet," from light beige to dark chocolate. The "sweeter" *miso* is usually best for the Western palate. The adventurous cook will find a world of interesting uses for this versatile and flavorful food (*see* p. 94).

momiji-oroshi: *see* p. 106.

ponzu sauce: *see* p. 99.

saké: Japanese *saké* (rice wine) should be available or can be ordered at any liquor dealer.

sanbai-zu: *see* p. 99.

sansho: A Japanese spice (*Xanthoxylum piperitum*). Powdered *sansho* is a pleasant addition to any spice shelf. Sometimes freshly ground black pepper can be substituted (*see* p. 106).

sarashi-negi: *see* p. 106.

sesame seeds (*goma*): There are two varieties, white and black (*see* p. 107).